I0062247

The Money Guide

Everything You NEED to Know About Money That You Didn't Learn at School

Saving, Investing & Growing Your Future!

by Larry Wallace

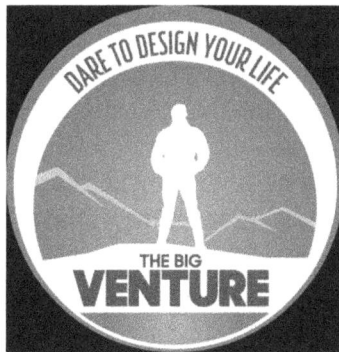

Copyright © 2017 By Larry Wallace
All rights reserved. No part of this book may be reproduced in any
form without permission in writing from the author. No part of this
publication may be reproduced or transmitted in any form or by any
means, mechanic, electronic, photocopying, recording, by any
storage or retrieval system, or transmitted by email without the
permission in writing from the author and publisher.
Larry@TheBigVenture.com.
Reviewers may quote brief passages in review.

Larry Wallace
TheBigVenture.com

Table of Contents

Who is this book for?

How to manage your money is one of the most important lessons anyone has to learn, which means that it's more than a pity – it's a national disgrace – that money management is something that is simply not taught in schools today.

School will teach you how to show respect to other people, how not to take advantage of superior strength if you have it, and how to conduct yourself politely in public. It will also make sure that, before you leave, you know about contraception and how to protect yourself and others against the tragedy that an unwanted child can be.

But what about the wanted child?

What about its future?

What about the well-being of the family?

Because, however much people like to tell you that money can't buy happiness, there isn't much doubt that the lack of money, or an inability to manage it properly, has been responsible and continues to be responsible for a great deal of the unhappiness at large in the world today.

So that is who this book is for.

It's about money – how to make sure you have enough, how to avoid being conned out of it, how to manage it so that it's always safe and yet it grows.

This book is for anyone who does not understand those things at the same deep level as they understand how to get up in the morning and go to bed at night.

In other words – this book is for YOU. I hope it will help contribute to your happiness and the happiness of your family.

What will this book teach you?

Money is at the heart of our world and everything we do in it.

Don't let forecasts of a cashless society change your view of that; money will still be central to the life of everyone. So, money is what this book will teach you about.

At the end of it you will have learned:

- Why money matters, what you can do with it, and how little you can do without it

- What makes money, money – where it gets its value from, how governments and central banks affect that, and what happens when either you or the country you live in doesn't have enough

- How we keep track of value between countries: what exchange rates mean

- The importance of living within your means, whatever they are

- Budgeting. Why it's so important, and how to do it

- The deadly trap of credit cards

- How to invest what you have left, whether it's peanuts or a fortune. Banks, stocks and shares, mutual and hedge funds, peer-to-peer lending

- What to do when you run out of money. How to strike a deal with your creditors, and what bankruptcy means

Introduction

Gary and Wayne are in their forties. They were born in the same hospital, went to the same schools, graduated high school at the same time. Neither of them went to college; both work with their hands – Gary is a drywaller and Wayne is a mason. Both married and have children.

Gary and his wife Lesley own their own house; while things were tough in the early years of their marriage, especially when the children were small and Lesley was not able to go out to work, they have come through that and now regard their life as comfortable.

Wayne and Joanna divorced, their marriage torn apart by money worries, and both now live separately in rented accommodation, though at bad times, Wayne has been known to sleep in his car for a few nights or even a few weeks at a time.

How did it get that way?

What did Gary know that Wayne did not? And where did he learn it?

They both went to the same schools at the same time and had the same teachers, so it can't have been there.

And maybe it should have been. Perhaps, if school had taught Wayne the lessons that Gary learned, Wayne and Joanna would today be like Gary and Lesley, comfortable in their pleasant home with their family around them.

In this book, we will discuss the lessons that Gary learned, but no one ever taught to Wayne.

Chapter 1: Does Money Matter?

Does money matter?

You could be excused for thinking that it did not, given the small amount of attention it gets at school.

High school graduates will have learned about algebra, about history, and about how to read a piece of fiction intelligently. And, of course, all of those things are important (though how much they will use algebra once they get into the wide world is anyone's guess).

Chances are, they'll have spent time learning to be tolerant of people with different worldviews, different sexuality, different ethnic backgrounds and different religions. Those things, too, are important.

But one of the things that will matter most for them in the years to come is money: what it is, what it can do for you, what it can do to you if you abuse it, and how to make the most of it. And about that, high school will have taught them nothing at all.

In the Introduction to this book, we talked about Gary and Wayne, and the different ways life is working out for them, and how different things might have been if Wayne had only been taught how to manage money differently.

It's never too late.

What I plan to do now is to deliver the lessons on money that should have been taught in high school. The earlier people get to these lessons, the better – but even much later in life, understanding money can change the way a person lives.

What you can do with money

1. Home

Everyone lives somewhere.

For the really unfortunate, "somewhere" can be a park bench, over a grille warmed by air from the kitchens below, or in store doorways when all the shoppers have gone home.

For others, it can be a mansion.

For both of those extremes, and for everyone in between, it is likely that money will have had a big say in the standard of accommodation they have.

2. Family

What it costs to raise a family depends to some extent on where you are and, also to some extent, on income levels (what, in some circles, would be described as social class, although that's not really accurate).

The US Department of Agriculture (and, no, we don't know any more than you do why it should be Agriculture that carries out this calculation) monitors child-rearing costs; the latest figures available are from 2013, at which time the Dept. of Ag said that to raise a child to the age of 18 in a middle-income family in America would cost just under $250,000.

It isn't actually that simple, because more than $70,000 of that figure was for housing, and the family is going to be paying housing costs in any case.

Nevertheless, even if you exclude that, you're still talking about $180,000 to age 18, which comes to a handy $10,000 a year. So, if you feel like raising the traditional average 2.4 child family, you'd better set aside $24,000 a year.

That's $2,000 a month. And it's coming out of taxed income. (I'll deal with the impact of tax on incomes later; for now, let's just bear in mind that there's a difference between the gross income on the job advert and the amount you see on your pay slip, and the difference goes to the government).

Having a family involves all sorts of costs. Some of them are optional. (The term normally used for the money that is left after you've met the costs you have to pay and out of which you can meet optional costs is discretionary income. Working out just how little of your overall income is discretionary can be a sobering experience for most people).

A family imposes obligations. All sorts of obligations.

Hazel and Jerome used to meet with friends most Saturdays; they'd have something to eat and then, over a beer in their favorite local bar, the men would watch baseball, or football, or hockey, or whatever happened to be on the widescreen TV at the time, while their wives shot the breeze about what had been happening in the past seven days.

Their first child was born on a Tuesday. It was an easy birth, and Hazel was home on Wednesday and up and around by Friday.

On Saturday, Jerome answered the phone. Would they be meeting the others in a couple hours? Jerome was about to say that, yes, of course they would – and then he saw the look on Hazel's face and realized that the days of those casual meetings were over, at least for the foreseeable future.

That's one example of how a family changes someone's life; there are many others.

When you live on your own, you can decide – within certain limits – how you want your life to be; when you will eat, where you will take your vacation, what you will spend your money on.

Marriage reduces the amount of choice in all those areas, and the arrival of children reduces it even more.

Responsible parents soon realize that they have an obligation to their children (who, after all, did not ask to be born) and that the obligation includes, among a number of other things:

- The obligation to put a roof over the family's heads and to feed and clothe them;

- The obligation to provide medical care;

- The obligation to make sure the children are educated, and educated to the highest level their intelligence and inclinations say they can reach.

There are other things that are not obligations – parents don't have to do them, and there will be times when it's in the interests of the children for parents not to do them – but they are real and they have an impact. Some of them are:

- To ensure that the family lives a life that all its members can join in. That includes weekend activities, trips to the theater and to sporting events, picnics;

- To pay sufficient attention to the children to know what they like to do and what they are good at and to do everything possible to make it possible for them to participate. That may involve buying sports equipment, driving the children to special educational and training events, paying a tutor to teach them the violin, and a host of other things.

What you can be certain of is that all those things will cost money.

Don't buy the old line that two can live as cheaply as one – and certainly don't buy the idea that the costs of raising a family are insignificant.

They *can* be insignificant, and for a number of families they are, but those families are the ones where the children are unhappy and the parents are unhappy. With themselves and with each other. You don't want to be part of that.

So: you want a family?

You want to raise children?

Better get serious, then, about looking after your money because if that family is going to be a happy one, the money is going to be spent on them, and not on you. Becoming a parent is not for the selfish.

Security

Security covers all sorts of things, but the security I'm speaking of here is not about keeping intruders out of the home, or preventing the car from being stolen. I'm talking about financial security.

In the early days of your working life, fresh out of school or college and earning for the first time, you can be a little lackadaisical about how much money is left at the end of the week, or the end of the month, or whatever period it is that you are paid for.

When your plans for the future start to crystallize, though – that's when you need to start taking care to make sure that there is enough money to fund what you want to do. I'm talking about saving.

There are a number of ways in which money can be saved, and you almost certainly should be adopting more than one of them.

I'll be talking later in the book about those various forms that saving can take; for now, the purpose is only to make sure that, when we do start talking about forms of saving, you understand why it's necessary. You can make all the plans you like, but if you run out of money at the wrong time, a lot of those plans will never happen.

"The rainy day"

The kind of security I was just talking about was the kind that makes sure you hold onto enough of your earnings to be able to fund the things you want to do in life.

There's another kind of security which is: how will you cope with a disaster?

You have a long drive to make, and your gearbox just blew up. There was a heavy storm and a tree in your garden fell on the house next door. The insurance company sent a lady round to look at it, and she says the tree was dying from the ground up, it was your job to see that and to get the tree cut down, you didn't – and so your insurance will not cover you. You walk out of the kitchen just for a moment, but then you see something interesting on TV and stop to watch it, forgetting that you have a frying pan over a lighted gas ring. Fire!

Those are all disasters.

What's worse: they are all potentially expensive disasters.

Everyone needs to have some money put away to help them deal with disasters exactly like that. The fact that at least nine people out of every ten DON'T have those rainy-day savings is neither here nor there; you need them, and if you don't have them, life will be that little less comfortable.

16

What you can do without money

2,200 years ago, the Roman playwright Plautus said, "The day, water, sun, moon, night – I don't have to purchase these things with money." (Not quite in those words, of course – he said it in Latin).

More recently, Billy Graham said, "The greatest legacy one can pass on to one's children and grandchildren is not money or other material things accumulated in one's life, but rather a legacy of character and faith."

And Margaret Walker said, "Friends and good manners will carry you where money won't go."

So, yes, it is true that there are things that money won't buy. It's also true that you need those things.

But, sadly, in the capitalist Western society that we live in (and don't be fooled – this is even more true in socialist countries in the East), you almost always need money before you can put yourself into a position to enjoy those things that money won't buy.

Nerds are the happiest people. Really?

A fellow writer has a son called Tom.

He says that Tom is a nerd, and that nerds are the happiest people, because they don't need money. I've met Tom and I understand why his father says what he does, but I'm afraid it doesn't hold water. What is true is that Tom is immune to the idea of what other people think about him.

Here's another quote: Will Rogers said, "Too many people spend money they earned to buy things they don't want to impress people that they don't like."

Tom would agree with that, and he only buys things he really wants. I've noticed that his wants are modest – and, yes, I would say he was happy. Unlike my friend, though, the conclusion I draw is not that nerds are the happiest people, but that the happiest people are those who don't feel obliged to spend money in order to impress other people. They only part with it when there's something they really want.

(And please note: that's twice I've used the word "want." I haven't used the word "need." I'll be talking later in the book about the difference between want and need.

Chapter 2: Where Does Money Get Its Value?

Money has a strange and interesting history.

Probably the first thing that had any value was the ability to work. If people wanted something, they paid for it with their labor. All sorts of things have stood in for money over the years – there was a time in the history of America when tobacco was money.

I'm not going to attempt to go into this in detail, because whole books twice as long as this one have been written just on the subject of what money is and what people have used to engage in financial transactions. (Cowrie shells, which were used in islands in the South Pacific for a time, are the example that every book and every article on the subject likes to refer to).

It has become popular in certain circles to answer the question, "How does a dollar bill get its value?" by saying that the value of a dollar bill or any other form of money comes either from government fiat – the government says, "That bill is worth a dollar," so a dollar is what the bill is worth, or by social convention – people are prepared to accept a dollar bill in return for a dollar's worth of services or goods, and so the bill acquires its value.

For the same reason as I don't want to go through the whole history of money – it would take more words than I plan to write – I'm not going to enter into all the pros and cons of this argument about where money's value comes from. It would simply take too long.

I am, though, going to say that I don't agree that the value of money comes either from government or from social convention. What lies behind the value of money is the knowledge that a government stands behind it and would, in the last resort, be prepared to substitute something that everyone would recognize as having value.

The something was usually either gold or silver.

If you picked up a British banknote and looked at it, you would see that it bears on its face a promise "to pay the bearer on demand" the face value of the note. Within living memory, that promise was rather longer, in that it promised to pay the bearer, should the bearer so request, the face value of the note *in gold*.

And gold, rather than tobacco or cowrie shells, has, in most of the world for most of the time, been the ultimate measure of value. Gold was held by central banks, and it was central banks that issued banknotes – so let's take a look at central banks.

Central Banks

The Federal Reserve is America's central bank, but every country other than the very smallest has one.

A central bank's functions are:

- To issue money and control the money supply

- To control interest rates

- (Usually) to oversee commercial banking in that country

- (Usually) to act as lender of last resort to the banking network in case of financial upheaval

The relationship between the central bank and the country's government varies; in some countries, the central bank is completely independent of government; in others, government has total control of the central bank.

It's likely that most central banks around the world are somewhere between those two points. Which brings us to:

Governments

I could write a whole book as long as this one on the subject of the different forms of government there are in the world, and the many ideologies that fuel them.

When we consider just how many different political viewpoints there are, it is amazing that almost everyone in the world believes that the system and the ideology that they grew up with is the most normal and obvious. Most of the trouble at present loose in the world probably comes from the clash between those many convictions.

Governments may be totalitarian or democratic (though every government of whatever hue claims to be democratic – it's a word capable of many interpretations). They may be dogma-driven or laissez-faire. They may be conservative, liberal, or libertarian (and don't ever make the mistake of imagining that liberal and libertarian are the same thing – they are poles apart).

Why do I spend a whole large paragraph talking about governments?

Because governments have everything to do with money.

And so they should, because one of the things that electors look to the government to do, when they go to cast their vote, is to make sure that the country avoids financial disaster.

In some countries, the central bank has such autonomy (is so independent) that government has virtually no say in how much money is circulating in the economy or on what the interest rates should be. But that is rare.

A government will usually have its hands on some, at least, of the levers of financial power. And government will almost always be the largest spender in the country, which means that, even if the central bank is completely independent, it has to look to government policy to decide just how much money needs to be in circulation and available.

Inflation and Hyperinflation

When economists use the word "inflation," they aren't talking about blowing up a balloon.

Inflation, in the way they use the word, means increasing prices. Of course, prices of different things rise at different rates, but in most countries an overall rate of inflation will be arrived at by taking account of price changes in a "basket" of products which, ideally, are chosen because of their significance in the lives of ordinary people.

The "rate of inflation" is the rate at which prices are rising over a given period – usually the 12 months preceding the point at which the rate of inflation is announced.

Hyperinflation is a great deal more serious than ordinary inflation.

Modest rates of inflation are not dangerous and can even be healthy for a country's economy, but hyperinflation happens when the value of a currency falls so fast that prices of even straightforward goods rise rapidly to a point where they are unaffordable by anyone but the very richest – or by foreigners.

America – or, at least, the South – experienced hyperinflation towards the end of the Civil War.

The Confederate dollar had been roughly equal to a US dollar throughout the war, but when people began to believe that the South had lost, they became reluctant to accept the Confederate dollar which, within a few days, went from being worth approximately one US dollar to a point where you needed 1,200 of them to buy a US dollar.

There have been many other cases of hyperinflation over the years; in Zimbabwe in 2008, prices were doubling every day, while in Hungary in 1946, a doubling of prices took only 15 hours.

Zimbabwe is as yet by no means out of danger. One of the most talked about hyperinflations was in Germany in 1923, and I'll deal with that in the next section.

Families who spend money they don't have go bankrupt. Can countries go bankrupt?

I'll be talking in a later chapter about bankruptcy and what it means to the individual or the family.

For now, I'll restrict myself to a definition of bankruptcy which is: an acceptance that the total debt exceeds the total assets and the income likely to be received in the foreseeable future, to a point where debtor and creditors must accept that the debtor is not going to be able to meet his or her financial obligations.

Individuals and families reach that position because they continually spend money they don't have. Governments, too, can spend money they don't have, raising the question: Can governments, too, go bankrupt? And the simple, though by no means exhaustive, answer is that it probably depends on the country.

Countries have certainly gone bankrupt in the past, and some seem determined to do so right now. And the citizens in a bankrupt country pay a terrible price for their country's default.

Rubbish piles up in the streets, because there is no money to pay the people whose job it is to remove it. People who work for the government – teachers, civil servants, nurses, doctors, the police and the army – starve, because there is no money to pay their wages. (The army, though, is not always subject to the same failure to pay as everyone else, because governments understand that, in the last resort, it will be the armed forces that keep them in power, and so they find the money from somewhere to pay the soldiers).

In the 1920s, Germany was completely unable to meet its financial obligations. In October 1923, when hyperinflation was at its worst, inflation was running at nearly 21% a day, which meant that it took less than four days for prices to double. Economic instability was followed by political instability, and it should be taken as a general rule that that will always happen.

The solution came from what some would see as a sleight of hand.

The Chancellor, Hjalmar Schacht, announced the introduction of a new currency, the rentenmark, to replace the existing mark. He said that the new currency would have an intrinsic value, because it would be secured on a mortgage over every asset in Germany. The words effectively meant nothing; people believed them because they wanted to believe them, and the German economy stabilized.

Historians, though, would say that that was not the end of the matter, because it can be argued that the financial agonies the German people went through in the 1920s led to the election of the National Socialist Party led by Adolf Hitler in the 1930s and the outbreak of the Second World War later in that decade.

Today, Zimbabwe and Nicaragua both suffer hyperinflation and their people are in desperate straits, while South Africa's currency is under great pressure and could slide into hyperinflation at any time.

The reason, in each case, is that all of those countries spend money they don't have and can't hope to earn. I'll have more to say on that in each of the next two chapters.

Well, fine. But what does that mean to you?

You can't do anything to reduce the risk Zimbabwe, Nicaragua and other countries run of bankrupting themselves. The risk you have to concern yourself with is much simpler than that.

It's the risk to you. The risk YOU run if YOU spend more than you earn for a prolonged period of time. And it isn't only you that runs that risk.

Your family shares it with you.

Chapter 3: Markers Of Value

Warren Buffett famously said, "Price is what you pay. Value is what you get."

And Karl Marx said, "Capital is money, capital is commodities. By virtue of it being value, it has acquired the occult ability to add value to itself. It brings forth living offspring, or, at the least, lays golden eggs."

Which tells you something about the difference between capitalism and socialism; the words of capitalist Warren Buffett are instantly understandable, while to Karl Marx we find ourselves saying, "What?"

Understandable or not, both of those quotations tell us something about the concept of value, but the most important lesson to learn is that value is not notional. Merely saying, "This is worth $5,000" won't make it so.

If you are the seller, what you have to sell is worth what you can get for it. If you are the buyer, what you want to buy is worth what you have to pay for it.

A couple days ago, I watched a webinar by someone who wanted to sell me some consultancy. He'd put together a package that involved me paying him some amount I can't remember now – about $2,500 – and, to persuade me, he'd assembled a bunch of "free" offers to go with it.

He listed them one at a time. "I put a value of $480 on this one, but you'll get it free as part of the package." "This, on its own, is worth $700 – but I'm throwing it in,

ABSOLUTELY FREE, as a welcoming gift when you sign up." And so on – you've probably heard or read similar claims yourself.

And the fact is that it doesn't matter what value he places on the first "free gift," or what he says the second one is worth – something is worth what you can get for it. (Personally, I would value all of his free gifts put together at about five bucks, but that doesn't matter – as long as enough people are convinced to buy the whole deal, he's doing okay).

That definition of value, which I admit is a lot shorter and a lot more straightforward than most of the textbooks will give you, is so important that I'm going to repeat it here:

> *If you are the seller, the value of what you have to sell is what you can get for it.*
> *If you are the buyer, the value of what you want to buy is worth what you have to pay for it.*

One more quotation. In his play, *Lady Windemere's Fan*, Oscar Wilde put these words into the mouth of his character, Lord Darlington: "a cynic is a man who knows the price of everything and the value of nothing."

I reproduce that here because I know that students who have had a serious grounding in English literature may well have been taught those words.

What saddens me is that they will almost certainly not also have been taught to apply them in general everyday use. Not in regard to the meaning of cynicism but to the concept of value. And that is at the heart of the rationale behind teaching those things about money that high school will not teach you.

There's one important measure of value that everyone needs to understand, and that is: exchange rates.

Exchange rates

If you ever leave your own country, on holiday or on business, or if you ever buy anything from another country, you are likely to come across the fact of exchange rates: that a currency used in one country is not the currency used in another country, and that you have to exchange the currency of your own country for the currency of the country you are travelling to or buying from.

The rate at which that exchange is carried out is known as the "exchange rate."

Exchange rates matter to different people for different reasons. Probably the most important global reason is that movements in a country's exchange rates reflect how that country is performing in world trade.

Take, for example, the exchange rate between the Canadian dollar and the American dollar. At the time I'm writing this (December 2016), one American dollar is worth CAN$1.34. That is, "snowbirds" travelling from Canada to, say, Florida in the next couple months to enjoy some sunshine and get away from freezing temperatures and snow will find that their Canadian dollars are worth a shade under 75 US cents when they go to buy gas or groceries.

There was a time in 2013 when the Canadian dollar was actually worth more than ("at a premium to") the US dollar, but since then it has been at a discount and the discount has been steadily growing.

Movements like that in exchange rates suggest that one country is doing better than the other economically. When you come right down to it, that means that the country whose currency is rising in value is selling to other countries more than it's buying from them (in products, in services, or both). And that's also how it is with families.

How much money a household has to spend at the end of the month, the end of the year, or at any other point in time is, when you come right down to it, simply a matter of: how much is coming in, and how much is going out?

Fixed and floating exchange rates

Everything I've said so far about exchange rates has assumed that the rate is free to float up and down according to the market's perception of where it should be.

Floating exchange rates are the most frequently found today among the major Western currencies, but that has not always been the case and is not the case in a number of countries today.

For example, both Saudi Arabia and the United Arab Emirates peg their currency (respectively the riyal and the dirham) to the US dollar.

Other currencies float, but in a hybrid sort of way because they are pegged against a basket of currencies that they deem suitable to them. There are regional currency unions which attempt to keep all the currencies of nations in line with each other (with results over the long term in which failure outruns success in the majority of cases).

The original peg was gold, and a currency was valued in terms of a specific weight of gold.

Since the price of gold was standard worldwide, that made it very easy to calculate the exchange rate between one currency and another, but pegs of that sort are very restricting and limit the monetary policies a country can adopt.

Most gold standards that survived into the twentieth century had been abandoned before that century had reached its halfway point.

Harold Wilson "The pound in your pocket"

A problem with fixed exchange rates is that they can make life very difficult for a country which is uncompetitive on the world stage.

With a floating exchange rate, the value of the currency would simply fall until it reached the level the market felt was justified, but when the exchange rate is fixed, that can't happen.

In the last resort, the country's central bank and/or government has to decide to devalue the currency – that is, to reduce the value represented by the fixed rate.

This led to one of the best-known errors of the spoken word by a politician in any country. The politician was Harold Wilson, who in 1967 was British Prime Minister.

The British pound had been trading for some time at a fixed rate of 2.80 to the US dollar. The American economy had outperformed the British economy (along with most other economies in the world at that time) and Britain could no longer sustain an exchange rate of 2.80.

Reducing the exchange rate was something Wilson did not want to do, because he saw it as an admission of failure by the British Labour government, but eventually he accepted that there was no choice and the rate was reduced to 2.40.

That was a sensible acceptance of reality on Wilson's part (though it would have been even more sensible to go to a floating rate, which, in due course, Britain did).

Unfortunately, though, the way in which he announced this move to the British people was far from sensible. He said, "Of course, the value of the pound in your pocket will not be affected." And the reason that that was far from a sensible thing to say was that, of course, the value of the pound in the pocket of the British people WAS affected.

Britain is a country that relies on international trade. It imports and exports a great deal – a far greater percentage of its GDP than, for example, America. A great deal of what the British people eat is imported. And what happens when you reduce the value of your currency is that the cost of what you import goes up.

So it came to be that "the pound in your pocket" became a byword for how politicians should not express themselves. On a par, in fact, with Hillary Clinton's acknowledgement that she had "misspoken" – and it would be easy enough to find equal verbal howlers by Republican politicians. Foot in mouth is a disease to which politicians are susceptible.

Chapter 4: Whatever Your Means, Live Within Them

Mr. Micawber is a character from Charles Dickens's novel, *David Copperfield*. He had a recipe for happiness: "Annual income twenty pounds, annual expenditure nineteen pounds, nineteen shillings and sixpence; result happiness. Annual income twenty pounds, annual expenditure twenty pounds and sixpence; result misery."

Dickens did not create this character out of his imagination only. He had experience of what happens when you live beyond your means, because that is what his father did.

Micawber could be said to be – and, in fact, probably was – based in large part on Charles Dickens's father who, as a result of spending more than he earned at a time when the law was much harder on those who failed to pay their debts, was in a debtors' prison at crucial times in the young Charles's life.

Today, not paying what you owe can result in bankruptcy but won't have you thrown into a debtors' prison – but it still stems from living beyond your means and it's still not a good idea.

It may seem as though spending money you don't have is the way to live your dreams, but the reality is the opposite. If you spend money you don't have, you *won't* get to live the way you dream of living. You will also, just like Mr Micawber, know what unhappiness really means.

This chapter is about some of the traps that lie in wait for you, and some of the ways to avoid them.

The need to plan. And that means budget

Preparing a budget can be a sobering experience. And that's the most important reason for doing it.

I talked in Chapter 1 about discretionary income – the amount you have left after you've paid everything you have to pay – and it's pretty well always less than you thought it would be. And that's true whether you earn $20,000 or $20 million a year.

So begin by making a list of all those things you have no choice but to pay. Some of them will almost certainly be on this list, but you will with equal certainty have others:

- **Housing costs.** This may be rent, mortgage payments, or something else, but most people are paying for the place where they live

- **Groceries**. I'm including in this everything you need to eat that you pay for yourself

- **Taxes.** Included in this are:

    - National income taxes such as those paid in America to the IRS

    - Local and state taxes such as property tax

Paying tax isn't optional, and too many people act as though it were. If you Google for a list of prominent people who have become bankrupt, you'll find that a very high proportion were put into bankruptcy by the IRS because they had neglected to pay their taxes. You don't want to add yourself to that number.

Never lose sight of the fact that your headline income (the gross amount the company pays you) and your take-home pay will only be the same if your gross income is so low that you don't pay any tax at all

- **Loan repayments.** You may have taken out a loan to buy a car or to pay for your education or healthcare costs. When you took the loan, you promised to repay it, almost always in regular monthly instalments. That promise has to be kept. Those payments are part of what you must take into account when you list your financial commitments in order to prepare your budget

Not on that list are things like trips to the movies, meals out, sporting events, holidays…that sort of expenditure can come to seem like an essential part of your life, but in fact it is discretionary.

You don't have to spend it, and the purpose of preparing this budget is to find out how much you have left – what your "discretionary income" is – after you've been paid for your work and have yourself paid everything you absolutely have to pay. Then you will know whether you can afford a week in the islands, or whether you'd better stay home for what has come to be known as a "staycation."

Learn to distinguish between "need" and "want"

This follows easily from the end of the last section, because when you are preparing your budget, the next thing you do after listing how much is in your pay packet after deductions, and how much of that money you have no choice but to spend, is to list the things that you would like to do and what they would cost.

Distinguishing between "needs" and "wants" is a lesson that parents have to teach their children at an early stage, because small children have difficulty in separating the two.

If they want something, then they need it. Don't let that difficulty follow you into adulthood. Beyond the basics of a roof over your head, food on the table and something to wear, almost every "need" is, in fact, a "want."

And what budgeting does is to help you understand just which of your wants can be satisfied this month – and which are going to have to wait, because you don't have the money for them yet. (Did someone mention credit cards? I'll come to that shortly).

Keep a record of what you spend. And that means *everything* you spend

Companies set budgets.

They may call it financial planning, or they may call it something else, but a budget is what it is. And then they keep track of how they are doing against the budget, and they do that by recording everything they spend.

They may have a whole finance department to do that; it may be a single person; in very small companies, it may occupy only part of one person's time, but it will be done. Every single cent that comes into the company, and every cent that goes out, is recorded with details of where it came from and what it represented.

Companies have to do that, because they are going to need to account to the tax authorities for their income and expenditure and because, unless the company is a sole trader, the shareholders or partners will need a clear and detailed explanation of the company's financial history and condition.

Have to or not, the fact is that companies are better run merely because they do keep a record of everything they spend and then look at the trends to see where they are off budget and where they are on – and you need to do the same.

Buy a notebook or open a spreadsheet on your computer and record where everything goes. And that's *everything*. If you're using a spreadsheet, you'll find it simple to use codes to indicate what you spend money on – 1 for accommodation costs, 2 for food, 3 for entertainment, and so on – making it much easier to see exactly what you are doing with your money, but even if you don't use codes, the record will still be very valuable. Notice that in that list I included both costs you must spend and your discretionary spending, and so should you.

Check the trends from time to time. That's why you have a budget – to see where you are exactly on target, where you are ahead of the game, and where you need either to reduce expenditure because you're exceeding budget or – if that simply isn't possible – how you need to increase the amount you budget for that cost.

Remember, though, that your total spend is limited by your net pay, so if one budget is increased, another has to be reduced.

Don't fool yourself. Don't set up the budget and tell yourself that you're doing fine because you've got a budget, even though you're not keeping within it. Take the budget figures seriously. It's your life.

Cash flow statement

The best way to keep track of your budget and how you are doing against it is by using a spreadsheet.

Spreadsheets will do all the calculations for you and, if you used the codes I suggested a little earlier, they will also allow you to do a quick analysis of how much you're spending and what you're spending it on as well as how much you're earning and what you're earning it for.

You can produce bar charts, pie charts and all sorts of other fascinating graphics to make the information clearer. But remember that that information and those graphics are only any use if you examine them to see what they are telling you.

When you prepare your spreadsheet, use columns for time (you can make that weekly, monthly, or whatever else seems right for your particular way of living) and use rows for types of income and types of expenditure.

Every time you commit yourself to a regular payment, enter it into the appropriate columns. If it's only a single payment, make sure it goes in the column that it should be in. The purpose of doing all of this is so that you can see at a glance whether you are going to have enough money each week or each month or each year to pay the things that you are obligated to pay.

It can also tell you when you have the money to buy something you want to buy, and when (and how much) you will be able to save – see the next chapter for suggestions on good places to save your money.

When you gamble, the house always has the advantage. Long term, the house wins. Which means you lose

The Great Wall of China was probably financed with lottery funds.

Lotteries were certainly being conducted in China at that time (4,000 years ago). Gambling may well go back even further than that. It certainly seems to be very deep rooted in the human psyche. At its worst, gambling can be an addiction every bit as bad as alcohol, but even when you have it less severely than that, gambling is an almost guaranteed way to lose money.

You can buy a ticket, go to a casino, bet on a horse race – there are many forms of gambling, but of one thing you may be certain: the house always wins in the end. And if the house always wins, then that means the gambler – you – must always lose.

Yes, you can have occasional wins, and they can feel great, and (and this may come as a surprise) the house is glad that you win – because that means you'll come back and bet some more, and they have enough experience to know that, in the end, the amount you lose will always be more than the amount that you won.

I'm not saying you should never buy a lottery ticket in a good cause. But think of it as a charitable donation, not as a gamble. (And stay inside your charitable donation budget figure).

Nor am I saying that you should never risk a little something on a horse owned by a friend or with a name that appeals to you. But do it in the knowledge that the odds are stacked against you.

Overall, your losses are going to be greater than your wins, so follow the basic rule of gambling and never, never bet more than you can afford to lose right now.

Credit cards: the dangerous honey trap

I said we'd come back to this subject.

Credit cards have their uses. They tell the seller you are who you say you are, they satisfy the seller that they'll be paid, and they provide a convenient way of making purchases without carrying around huge amounts of cash. And all of that is great – so long as you pay the balance down to zero at the end of each month when you get the bill.

The interest rates charged on credit cards are high. The interest rates charged on certain credit cards are outrageous. The only people who charge higher interest rates than credit card companies are loan sharks. Many people would say that it isn't easy to tell loan sharks and credit card companies apart. I'm not sure that I would want to argue very hard with that.

In the next chapter, I'll be talking about saving, and one of the subjects I will cover is compound interest.

Compound interest is a wonderful thing – for the saver (or, it was, when savings accounts were still paying rates of interest that were not completely laughable).

For the borrower, it's quite dreadful. And compound interest – interest on interest – is what you are paying when you don't pay off your credit card bill each month.

The interest rate you pay on your credit card is called the APR and, in America at the moment, for the most part it varies between 13% and 22%. If you miss a payment, then the interest rate increases to what credit card companies themselves call a penal rate – to most people, 13% to 22% looks fairly penal as it stands, a time when you will be lucky to receive 1% on balances you hold in the same bank's savings accounts.

Before you buy something with a credit card knowing that you're not going to be able to pay off the whole amount at the end of the first month, give some thought to how much the purchase is going to cost you in total. I'm going to give you two examples.

First, suppose you buy something for which the purchase price for cash would be $1,000 and you pay for it with a credit card bearing the interest rate 15%, following which you pay off the credit card debt in equal monthly instalments over five years. By the end of the five years, that $1,000 purchase will actually have cost you $1,437. Unless of course you missed a payment, and then penal rates will have added to the cost.

Second, the same $1,000 purchase when the interest rate is 22% and the loan (because that's what it is) is paid off over two years would mean a total cost of $1217.

And the reality is that for most people the transactions are never that simple.

Most credit cardholders will not get to the end of paying for the first item without adding something else on their card.

Some people actually spend their whole lives with their credit cards "maxed out" and that means that a huge part of their monthly income or weekly income is not spent on something they want but merely goes to meet interest payments.

So treat credit cards with great caution, and always try to use some other form of finance if you know you're not going to be able to pay for this purchase at the end of the month.

And – and I'm sorry if this seems like the sort of thing a killjoy would say, but it's true – the best kind of financing for most of the things that go on people's credit cards is to save the money until you can pay cash for it. Then ask for a discount for cash. If you don't get it, you don't get it, but it's amazing how often you can strike a deal.

Develop immunity to advertising

Advertising is there to sell goods and services.

Obviously.

What the advertiser hopes is that the money spent on advertising will come back many times over in profit on the sale. The agency handling the advertising works for the company that has something to sell, and not for the buyer. If you are the buyer, the advertising agency is emphatically not on your side.

I'm not going to suggest that most advertising is untruthful, because there's a lot of legislation around now that prevents some of the more outrageous misrepresentations that were seen in the past. But things are certainly presented in the best possible light, and possible drawbacks may not be drawn to your attention.

An acquaintance of mine is a copywriter and he recently prepared some advertising for a WordPress plug-in that did a particular job (and, apparently, did it well). "So," I said, "you'd recommend that plug-in, would you?"

"No," he said. "I wouldn't. Because what it doesn't tell you there is that the plug-in doesn't work on its own. Once you've paid for that and downloaded it, you'll find out in the installation instructions about the other plug-in you need. Which costs three times what this one does."

What I loved about that was the way he said, "what it doesn't tell you," when what he really meant was, "what I have chosen not to say." I braced him with that and he looked at me as though I had lost my senses. "But I work for the guys who write the plug-in," he said.

Bear that story in mind when someone, through advertising, is trying to persuade you to buy something. Check it out. At the very least, look for some reviews, and don't look for them on the company's own website. One of the benefits of the Internet today is that there are lots of independent sites running reviews of all sorts of products.

Chapter 5: Forms Saving Can Take

You've set up your budget so that you'll have money left over at the end of each month. Unless you're planning to keep it under the mattress, the money has to go somewhere.

Most often, unless you are paid in cash and you cover your bills in the same way, the money will already be in the bank, almost certainly in a current account, and what you need to decide is: are you going to leave it there, or find somewhere else to keep it?

You do need to keep some money readily available, because from time to time there are going to be bills you have to pay. It's also true for most people today that they have regular commitments that are going to be covered by automatic PayPal payments or by direct debits and you don't want a nasty surprise when one of those results in you being unexpectedly overdrawn.

Most banks today charge penal rates of interest as well as a hefty service charge any time someone goes into unauthorized overdraft. They'll never admit it, but the banks actually love it when you do that because they're not going to lose the money (if they thought there was the remotest chance of that, you wouldn't have been allowed to overdraw in the first place) and they hit you with that delightful (to them) charge and interest rate.

This can seem tedious, but whenever you sign a direct debit or authorize PayPal to make regular payments on your behalf, you should take note. Enter it into the spreadsheet I talked about in Chapter 4. If it's a recurring payment, make sure it's in every column it needs to be in.

Now: what are you going to do with money that you don't need to keep immediately to hand?

Banks and similar institutions

One place you can keep your money is in the bank, credit union, building society or similar institution.

There was a time when doing that was financially rewarding, because you got a good interest rate, and that may be true again at some point in the future, but right now interest rates are lower than they have been in living memory and there's very little financial reward from putting your money into a bank savings account. (I hesitate to say that interest rates are as low as they can go, even though in many banks they are now 0%, because banks are already talking about negative interest rates – that is, if you put money into a savings account in a bank, instead of the bank paying you interest on the money, they charge you what is effectively a negative interest rate for looking after it on your behalf).

There is, then, very little point in keeping much money in a bank savings account, but it is a good idea to keep a little there has a "buffer."

The idea of a buffer is that, occasionally, however well you plan, unless you are keeping far too much money in your current account, you are going to overdraw. When that happens, you have a number of hours to put your account in order without having to pay a penalty. (If your bank doesn't give you those few hours, you're banking with the wrong people – find one that does). If you have buffer account, you can do a quick transfer – provided that the savings account where you keep your buffer money allows immediate withdrawals. If it doesn't, find one that does.

Personally, I'm a believer in having an account with more than one bank. We think of banks as pillars of rectitude, integrity and honesty.

It's an old-fashioned view that no longer holds water. Almost everything a bank does in its day-to-day dealings with ordinary people like you and me is decided, not by a person, but by a computer. Some of those actions are hair-raising.

To take one example that I was aware of recently, a bank customer on holiday in another country rented a car from a car rental firm that was large and well-known but, at least at that branch in that country, had been responsible for a number of fraudulent transactions on a customer's credit card.

So, what did the bank do? Did it inform the customer – its own customer – that they were dealing with a company that could not be trusted? No. What it did was to suspend all transactions on the customer's account, and on the customer's credit card. It did that without informing the customer, who only discovered that something was wrong when checking into a hotel that could not take money from his credit card.

And that is why I believe in having accounts with more than one bank. It crossed my mind that I might provide you with a list of banks that were totally trustworthy, but I realized after a little thought that I would have to leave the page blank.

The Stock Exchange

It would be possible to write a book twice the length of this one on the subject of investing in companies through the medium of the stock exchange.

I simply don't have room to do that, so I'm going to restrict myself to saying that buying and selling shares is not just for the wealthy or for those who have a deep knowledge of company finance and that, while you do have to take care to protect yourself, you are by no means as much at risk as you can be in, say, Forex trading or derivatives.

You need a registered broker. Find one yourself – make it a policy never to take advice from or do business with someone who contacts you by phone, and take a great deal of care in verifying the credentials of anyone who writes to you. In the old days, you could simply ask your bank manager for a recommendation, but that is much less sound as a policy now.

It isn't really that you need to exercise due diligence if you get a phone call from someone who wants to be your broker. It's more a simple statement of fact that the chances of such a phone call coming from someone who is honest are vanishingly small. Almost all such calls (shading into all such calls) are scams. Protect yourself by having nothing to do with them.

Find a broker by online search in a market close to you. Then check out the broker's antecedents and reputation. There will be a website. How big is this firm and how long has it been in business? Is there any negative sentiment about the firm online? Do they act as market-makers, and if so, for whom? And does the website give an address? If so, are you close enough to walk by and make sure that the office is really where they say it is? Then why not walk in and say you'd like to talk to someone about opening an account?

On that question of addresses, by the way, when I talk about forex trading I shall saying that one of the ways to detect a scam is: do they have an address on their website? Is it one that can be checked? That should be an automatic test for anything to do with money. If the website doesn't tell you precisely where people are, precisely who the people in charge are, and precisely how to go about getting your money back in the case of disaster, then you are probably looking at a scam.

A decision you have to make at a very early stage of share dealing is: are you investing for growth, or for capital income? Generally speaking, you can't have both. If you're relatively young, and you want to put some money away for a child's education, for your old age, or both, then what you are after is growth. If you're past retirement age, you have money to invest, and you want to get the best income you can from it, then income becomes what you want.

Don't be distracted from that target. And remember that there are no easy pickings. If anyone promises you double-figure growth in a year or two, there are two things you need to do. The first is to ask yourself why this is being offered to you and why the person doing the offering is not keeping it for their personal gain? And the second is to walk away. Find someone else.

You have to decide what shares you are going to invest in. To do that, you will have to learn – if you don't already know – how to read a balance sheet and a profit and loss account, but the single most important document you need to read is the cash flow statement. It tells you what money has come into the company and from where; what money has gone out of the company and for what; and how much is left.

The reason this is so important is that financial statements can and do lie. They are manipulated and presented by people who do nothing else and a story that is actually disastrous can be made to look like the success of the year – and this applies to the biggest, best reputed and most successful companies and not just to the charlatans. But cash does not lie.

If the company claims to have made a profit of $50 million and is seeking to raise $100 million as a cash injection, you must ask why, and you do that by examining the cash flow statement. There may be perfectly good reasons. The company may have an excellent opportunity to invest – in a new company, in a new product, or in a myriad other ways – but you need to know what it is and you need to decide whether it satisfies you. If not, forget about it. There will be other opportunities: other companies in which you can invest with a feeling of security.

You will get plenty of advice on what to buy. If you signed up with a broker, the broker will produce research reports which, at a price, they can make available to you. Find out whether there is a connection between the broker and a company in which they are suggesting you invest. If there is, find out the precise nature of the connection.

You will get emails telling you that a particular company is about to double the money of anyone fortunate enough to hold its shares. The emails come from someone you never heard of, and I suggest you keep it that way. Ignore those emails. Just as you should ignore the phone calls from people who want to know how you are and are so pleased to have this opportunity to tell you about this great purchase they are able to recommend. They will do very well out of any investment you make; you won't. Ignore the phone calls.

One very popular line is from the caller who tells you that he works for a firm that was retained by a listed company to carry out a confidential research project into the company's prospects. The report is now ready; it's not going to be released to the general public but a select few, of whom you are fortunate enough to be one, can be told the headlines and will have the opportunity to buy shares at what, as soon as the information becomes generally known, will be a knockdown price.

If you get a call like that, be aware that stock exchanges are as close to a perfect market as it is possible to be. A perfect market is one in which all stakeholders have the same information at the same time.

A company that had actually done what this person is claiming it has done, commissioning a research project of which the results will be told only to a few, would be breaking the law and its directors would be liable to be banned from holding office for a number of years. That's true in America, it's true throughout Europe, it's true in Australia and New Zealand – it's simply true. So, if someone makes a call like that, laugh and hang up.

Something else you might find wise is not to invest in businesses you know nothing about. How will you know if you're being spun a line?

As I've said, I don't really have space to go into all of this in great detail. One day, I'll write an investment book, and everything anyone needs to know will be in there, but I can't see that coming in at less than 40,000 words, so there just isn't room to do it here.

Mutual Funds

If you lack confidence to plow your own furrow in buying and selling shares, you may want to take a look at mutual funds

A company already established in the finance industry sets up a fund in which members of the public become shareholders. The fund will have a declared objective, which will vary widely from fund to fund, so it's advisable to look at the objectives of a number of mutual funds and decide which one has objectives that most closely match your own. (You still need to look at the track record and credentials of the fund management team and company, but finding one that wants to do what you want to do is a start).

The mutual fund invests the money it receives from shareholders in securities, and not just any security. It can buy stocks, money market instruments, and bonds, and before deciding that a mutual fund is for you, you should take a close look at the kind of security it invests in and decide whether you're happy with investments in that field.

The attraction of a mutual fund for investors is that you are getting the investment expertise and knowledge of a professional team, for which you are paying a fee that is proportional to your investment in the fund – if you have a hundredth of 1% of the value of the fund, you will pay a hundredth of 1% of the fees.

Mutual funds are closely regulated, which should give some feeling of confidence to the less knowledgeable investor, but that confidence should be tempered by the fact that the close regulation exists because of a number of scams that have damaged the reputation of mutual funds over the years, and the knowledge that, where so much money is gathered together in one fund, there will the vultures be, also. It seems that humankind is endlessly inventive when it comes to finding ways to deprive other people of their money through dishonest means.

What I'm saying is that there have been scams in the past and there will be scams in the future. By and large, the mutual funds in regulated existence today are honest, but the investor is never freed from the obligation to examine continually the nature of the investments being made on her or his behalf and to question any "innovative" way of doing business that may be suggested.

It may be a brilliant idea that is both safe and completely legal. It may also be a snare that the regulators have not yet identified for what it is, and which they may continue not to see until disaster has struck.

In other words, the old Latin tag, *caveat emptor* (buyer beware) applies here as in everything to do with saving and investment.

Most mutual funds are open-ended, which means that there is no limit to the number of investors or the amount invested, and the fund will always be prepared to sell new shares to new investors or existing shareholders who want top up their holding.

When you want your money out, you sell the shares back to the fund. The price at which you buy and sell is fixed each day at the close of trading when the fund manager calculates the net asset value (NAV) of the total of assets held by the fund and divides that figure by the total number of shares in existence. The price of a stock can fluctuate wildly during the day; that does not happen with mutual funds.

Note that when I said you sell your shares back to the company I was missing out a step for the sake of simplicity. It's true that, for some funds, you buy and sell in direct dealings with the fund, but usually transactions take place through a third party who might be a broker, a bank, or some other financial intermediary.

I hope by now I don't need to remind you to be as cautious about the integrity of the third-party to whom you are entrusting your money as you should be about the fund itself. There are some 600 intermediaries, so you should be able to find one that you feel able to deal confidently with.

The same wide availability is true of the funds themselves. America has more than 8,000 mutual funds that are publicly traded. More than 4,000 of them invest in equities, more than 2,000 in bonds, roughly 1,000 in money market instruments, and the rest are hybrids dealing in two or more of those investment fields.

I, personally, would not dream of investing in any fund where any of the people involved – as managers, as advisers, or in any other capacity – had ever been in trouble with the regulatory authorities. I am aware, though, that other people feel happy to take that risk in exchange for a higher return.

The rule here is the same as in any other form of investment: only you can decide what level of risk you are happy with – but remember that you are exposing your family to the risk, too.

If you're not in America, or even if you are but feel like investing in some other English-speaking country to take advantage of opportunities in British, Australian, New Zealand or some other similar market, remember that mutual funds there are called unit trusts.

Hedge Funds

A hedge fund is similar to a mutual fund, but subject to different regulation.

The critical regulatory difference is that anyone can invest in a mutual fund, but the kind of security in which the mutual fund can invest is restricted. A hedge fund, on the other hand, can invest in anything it chooses, but the people who can invest in it are restricted.

The basic assumption is that investors in hedge funds are "sophisticated" investors, with experience that will allow them to protect themselves. Current regulations say you need an annual income of at least $200,000 before you can become a hedge fund investor.

I'm not going to say a lot more about hedge funds because the fact is that, if you have access to a hedge fund, you probably don't need this book. What I will say is that some hedge funds have made a killing in forms of security that would scare the pants off the average investor – and a large part of that killing ends up in the pockets of the managers of the funds (20% of the fund's annual profits traditionally belongs to the fund manager).

However, if you want to take a punt on a fund that invests in companies that are in trouble, because it believes it has the management expertise to turn it around, then this may be the right sort of vehicle for you. (That's not the only kind of hedge fund there is, and in fact it probably accounts for less than 15% of those that are out there).

You can also be confident that there are some big names in this field – Warren Buffett and George Soros, to name only two, and both of them have been known to return around 30% profit to their investors, though that was in what were unquestionably boom years.

Investing in Forex and Derivatives

Forex stands for "foreign exchange." I've already talked about exchange rates and what they are, and exchange rates can vary widely and wildly.

The underlying trend in Forex has to do with trading conditions between nations, but a lot of other factors, some short-term and some not, will affect the value of one currency in terms of another. A recent example was the vote by the British people to leave the European Union.

This decision, which is known as Brexit, caused the British pound to fall in value against most other major currencies. Whether that was the right decision for the market to make will not be known for two, three, or even more years, while other fluctuations in exchange rates are done and dusted within 24 hours.

There are many ways to invest in foreign exchange movements and my advice to most readers of this book is: Don't. I know that you have read all sorts of claims in emails, on Facebook and Twitter, and in advertisements in specialized journals from people claiming to have made thousands of dollars a week by sitting in their bedroom, trading on a laptop. I doubt that one in a thousand of these claims is true.

Just ask yourself: if you had developed a piece of software capable of analyzing in real-time movements in a number of currencies in relation to each other and, as a result of that analysis, showing you how to place a bet (because that is what it is) on what happens next to a pair of those currencies in such a way that over any period of time you will make an absolute fortune – then what would you do? Would you run the software, place the bets, and rake in those vast profits? Or would you share the software with other people? Got the answer? Right.

Now you know why I say that those offers are scams. Very well-funded scams. Very well presented scams. But why not? The people involved in them are making a lot of money from gullible people. Why would you not expect them to have invested in impressive websites?

And who are those people? It says in the ad that they have many years of experience in Forex investment. Great – but why aren't they named? And why do those websites never – ever – give a physical address that tells you where they are and that can be checked? That is one of the most common scam alerts.

People will go on running these scams, and other people will go on falling for them. Don't be one of those mugs.

As for derivatives, do you remember Lehmann Brothers? They were founded in 1850. They were the fourth largest investment bank in America. They employed some of the most knowledgeable analysts and traders in the world. They knew far more about derivatives than you or I will ever learn. And in 2008, they were bankrupted. By derivatives. If they didn't know what they were doing how likely is it that you and I will do better?

My own approach, when someone tries to sell me any kind of derivative, is to say, "Just explain to me how that works." And after they have spouted meaningless drivel for a couple of minutes, I say, "I'm sorry. I never buy anything from someone who can't explain what it does and how it works." And that should be an unbreakable investment rule for you. If you don't understand it, don't buy it.

Peer-to-peer lending

Banks no longer pay interest rates that make it worth depositing money with them. And yet, people are still borrowing money.

Peer-to-peer lending brings together people who have savings on which they would like to earn a return and people who want to borrow money. It takes your money and splits it up among a number of borrowers.

If, for example, you deposit $1,000, the peer-to-peer lender may divide that over 50 separate loans, putting $20 of your money into each one. Someone borrowing $10,000 may have that loan put together from the deposits of 500 savers.

If the loan goes bad, the depositors whose money made up that loan lose all of it – but a good peer-to-peer lending operation is very cautious about the credit rating of the people it lends to, and depositors can at present expect to earn 3% to 4% on their savings and for losses to be rare.

That's a brief explanation of peer-to-peer lending; you've read enough of this book to know that I would recommend that you inspect the lender's record with care. You should also follow the "eggs in baskets" rule by spreading all of your savings and investments over a number of homes so that you don't lose the lot in one dreadful event.

Chapter 6: What To Do If Disaster Strikes

Anyone can get into financial difficulty. And I do mean anyone.

You doubt that? Well here are a few people who went bankrupt before making it big: Henry Ford. Walt Disney. Colonel Sanders. Milton Hershey. Donald Trump. HJ Heinz. And – wait for it, wait for it – Abraham Lincoln. In fact, Lincoln was bankrupt twice and Disney a few times more than that.

So bankruptcy is not a disgrace, and nor will it prevent someone from being successful in the future. Bankruptcy is not, though, a painless way out; in fact, it's anything but.

Bankruptcy hurts. You won't be able to get credit, your bankruptcy will be on your record and very public, most of what you earn as a bankrupt will be taken to set against your debts, and until you are discharged (which does not, as some people think, happen automatically, and will depend on your attitude to your creditors and to your debts), what you can do will be seriously limited. Some professions will not be open to you, and there are some that you might already be in that will show you the door when your bankruptcy is announced.

Don't think of bankruptcy as an easy escape from a mess you happen to have got yourself into. It isn't that – it's a last resort that will give you an opportunity, eventually, to start your life again free of debt.

And when that happens, I hope you will have adopted a different attitude to credit.

Striking a deal with your creditors

The first thing to do if you find yourself in a position where you can't pay your debts as they fall due is to try to negotiate a deal with your creditors. Don't just ignore them, and don't try to run away from them – they'll find you.

In the nineteenth century, it was possible for people to conduct two or more wholly separate lives, with the people they knew in one life having no idea that the other life existed. That became more difficult in the twentieth century, especially in the second half, and today it is impossible.

If someone wants to find you, they will. It's only in the more extreme cases that they even need to hire a private eye to do it. And, once they see that you have tried to run away or otherwise to avoid the fact that you owe them money, they are liable to take quite a hard line.

But most creditors will have at least a degree of common sense and, if they see that you are trying to cooperate and find a way out of your predicament, they are more likely to help. Not because they are decent human beings, but because they can't see any other way to get their money back.

Unless you are an old hand at this, you will probably need assistance. There is almost bound to be a not-for-profit debt relief agency near you who will assign a counselor to talk you through what you need to do and how to do it.

The counselor won't do it for you, but can provide advice, show you how to make contact, help you draft letters in the form that will be most acceptable to the people you send them to, and keep your morale up when it sags.

When you meet your counselor, but before you make contact with any of your creditors, decide what it is you're going to ask for. There are a number of alternatives:

- Reduction in interest rate

- A "holiday" – a period during which you won't be required to make payments

- Debt settlement, by which I don't mean payment in full – I mean that you offer a partial payment, on condition that it is accepted as full payment and the remainder of the debt is written off.

Sam Goldwyn famously said that a verbal contract wasn't worth the paper it was written on. That also applies to verbal agreements with creditors. Whatever agreement you come to, you need it in writing.

The first thing to be aware of is that the person you get hold of when you telephone may not have authority to agree something with you. Indeed, that person may be paid on results, and may have a strong personal financial interest in getting you to pay something off the debt.

If so, rest assured that you will be told that a part payment is being sought to show your willingness to cooperate, even if the real reason is to earn a bonus for the person you're speaking to.

One reason why anyone who is not a seasoned negotiator will need assistance is that the two sides to this conversation – you and the creditor – have very different objectives. If you are honest with yourself, you really want to get the amount you owe reduced. You've been too profligate with your money.

Or, actually, you haven't – you been too profligate with somebody else's money, and now they want it back and that's a problem for you. Or you've been careful with money, but something disastrous has gone wrong (between 60% and 75% of all personal bankruptcies in America are caused by medical debts – that is, money owed to hospitals and doctors.

Unless you planned to get ill, or be in an accident, or (worse) have one of your children involved in an accident, and unless the plan included making yourself unable to earn a living, those debts were nothing to do with your carelessness. But you still owe them, and you can still go bankrupt because of them).

So, you're on one side and a creditor or a bunch of creditors is on the other. You want to see the debt seriously reduced or even written off so that you can get on with your life; they want all their money back. That's the place you start from.

They are more likely to be ready to grant you a reduction in interest rates or a payment holiday, or just to agree to hold off taking you to court for a while, than they are to agree to some kind of write-down or write-off. What you most want is what they don't want, and what they most want is what you don't want. For most people, life will be easier with someone in their corner who's been down this road before.

Timing is important. It's fairly pointless even to make the first contact to begin negotiation until you've missed three payments, so long as you take note of what I said earlier and don't do anything that makes them think you're hiding or running away.

A phone call – or, better still, an email or letter – saying that you're very sorry to be behind but you hope to catch up soon is a good idea. Just so that they know that you're the kind of responsible person who doesn't run away from debts.

But something happens to most credit card debts after six months of non-payment: the credit card company sells them on to a debt collection agency. That – just before the six months are up – is going to be the best time to make a very serious attempt to get your debt cut.

Think about it: the credit card company is going to package all of its six month overdue debts together and offer them to a collection agency. Just like, a few years ago, the banks sold off all their dud mortgages. (You thought you'd be alone in being overdue with your credit card company? Dream on. The banks issued far too many cards, and set the credit limits for too high, in exactly the same way as they lent too much money to people who wanted to buy a house but couldn't afford it. For some time now, they've been paying the penalty).

The collection agency will look long and hard at each of the cases they are being offered and then make an offer based on how much, realistically, they think they'll be able to recover by making themselves extremely unpleasant to the debtors.

There will probably be some that they know from the start will be hopeless cases – they'll be lucky to recover five cents in the dollar. There will be others from whom they think, in time, they can probably get the lot back. That doesn't mean they'll offer to pay the bank the full amount it is owed. If they do believe they'll make full recovery, they'll probably offer the bank about 50% of the amount due.

So why wouldn't the bank take 50% from you, and save themselves the trouble of offloading this debt to an agency?

It won't be as simple as that – they won't just say, "Oh, okay then," to an offer of 50% of the debt you've run up. "You cannot be serious," is a more likely response. But they are realists and they'll be thinking about the offer.

It's important at this stage that you be honest. If you have a good reason for being in so much debt that you can't pay it off (like the medical expenses I mentioned earlier), then tell them about it. Anything you can say that reinforces the idea that you are not a professional debt-dodger but an honest citizen who hit a patch of bad luck will help.

Never lose sight, though, of the other side's aims. They want repayment, and if they think there is some likelihood of collecting down the road, that's what they'll hold out for.

So let them know what the alternative is. But don't threaten. "Accept 40%, or I'll go bankrupt," is not a good idea, because:

a) People don't like being threatened, they react badly to it, and the person you are speaking to has almost certainly had this sort of conversation many times – and you haven't; *and*

b) It will cause the person you are speaking to to doubt your integrity.

Much better would be something like, "I've thought about bankruptcy, and everyone is advising me to go bankrupt, and I guess I may have to in the end, but I really don't want to. It feels like a terrible thing to do and I'd like to avoid it if I can. But I just can't pay this debt as it stands." When you say that, ooze sincerity. As any politician will tell you, "Sincerity is the thing. If you can fake that, you can fake anything."

Don't let me give you the idea that it will be easy. It won't.

When you raise the possibility that if your offer is not accepted you will go bankrupt, what you are telling the bank is: "I owe you money. I can't pay it all, but I'm offering some. If I go bankrupt, you may get nothing at all. So, which would you rather have? Some cake? Or crumbs on a plate?"

The drawback, of course, is: you have to have some money to make good on your offer. And this also applies to a debt management plan, or DMP. So let's look at that.

Debt Management Plan (DMP)

If you're in the kind of debt problems that got you avidly reading this chapter, your debts are probably not restricted to one credit card. Chances are, you owe money to a number of people.

What you need to do (and you will almost certainly need a credit counselor to help you with this) is to put together a deal that all of your creditors will accept. The terms of the deal will be that everyone accepts something that the World Bank has been calling a "haircut."

Everyone agrees to accept a percentage of the money that they are owed as full settlement – once they have the money, you owe them nothing more. So, if you owe a total of $100,000 and you agree a DMP that obliges all creditors to accept a 50% haircut, then after you've paid $50,000, you walk away debt-free.

The drawback is the one I referred to a moment ago – you need to have the $50,000 to offer, or at the very least you need to have a significant chunk of it. If you say, "I'll pay you $50,000, but it will take me 10 years to do that in equal monthly instalments, and right now I don't have anything, so I'd like to start the repayment schedule one year from now," you are offering a deal they probably won't accept. It's important that you be able to come up with, at the very least, a significant down payment, and if you can pay the whole lot in one sweep, so much the better.

Why do I keep referring to this as a drawback? For three reasons. One is obvious: you have to have that money in the first place. The second is that you have to tell your creditors you have it. And that could lead to unpleasant action on their part. *Which is why you need a counselor who has negotiated these deals in the past and can help you now.* And the third is that a great many DMP's that are agreed are never completed. Here's what happens in a typical case.

You owe $100,000. You can raise $15,000 in cash, and so you offer a deal whereby everyone settles for 50% to be paid with the $15,000 cash and the balance at $100 per month which you will hand to the counselor and the counselor will distribute among your various creditors.

You have to agree that you will not borrow any more money during the repayment time, and you have to surrender all of your credit cards. You've actually been given a good deal, but too many people don't see it that way. They got into a mess in the first place because they like to spend money, even when they don't have it, and they want to go on spending money they don't have. So, the DMP breaks down. When that happens, the option you are left with is bankruptcy.

Bankruptcy

I've already said that this is the last resort, but I'll say it again: whatever you might have been told, bankruptcy is the last resort. But sometimes, it's unavoidable.

If you decide that this is your only way out, then get a lawyer. Not a credit counselor; a lawyer. And one with experience in handling bankruptcies.

Bankruptcy usually starts with a petition presented to the bankruptcy court by the debtor – that's you. Petitions can be presented by corporations, but company bankruptcies and personal bankruptcies are two different things. There has been a change in emphasis in the law on bankruptcy and the way bankruptcy is handled.

For many years, the accent was increasingly on giving relief to the debtor. That was good – it was humane – but it became clear that a number of people were taking advantage of creditors by borrowing money that they could never hope to repay and then choosing bankruptcy as a way of getting out from under the load of all that debt. Law and practice were changed to make that a little harder, and you can now expect the courts to be a little more judgmental in how they deal with you.

There is a US Bankruptcy Code, and it is federal courts that apply it. The code has a number of chapters, of which Chapter 7, Chapter 9, Chapter 11, and Chapter 13 are significant in that they refer to different kinds of bankruptcy.

I'm not going into them all here, because I would rapidly use up another fifty pages. As I said, find a lawyer who deals with bankruptcy, and be prepared to listen as he runs through all the reasons why bankruptcy may not be the best idea for you. In the end, the decision will be yours and you will instruct the lawyer accordingly.

Conclusion

The reason for writing this book was to make good the gaps in the education system.

Money, what it is, how to use it, and what to do when things go wrong, are vital life lessons. They should be taught in school, but they are not. I hope you will feel I have gone some way to correcting that omission here.

There is an old saying that, "Money is a good servant, but a bad master." What I have set out to do is to provide in this book enough information on how to make money your servant, and also enough on what to do if money has become the master.

If I have one wish, it is that everyone who reads this book will close it at the end with the feeling that they have learned a number of lessons, of which the most important is that spending money you have not yet earned has, for many people, been a route to disaster, but that you now have the tools to live your life in control of your finances and – and one follows from the other – in control of your own happiness.

Thank you for reading to this point. I wish you all success in your life.

Final Words

I would like to thank you for purchasing my book and I hope I have been able to help you and educate you on something new.

If you have enjoyed this book and would like to share your positive thoughts, could you please take 30 seconds of your time to go back and give me a review on my Amazon book page!

I greatly appreciate seeing these reviews because it helps me share my hard work!

Again, thank you and I wish you all the best!

Disclaimer

I have created this book with the purpose to provide information on money management.

It is sold with the understanding that the author and publisher are not engaged in any sort of professional services or legal advice.

Every effort has been made to ensure this book is complete and without error, however, it's possible that there may be errors, whether in content or other.

Therefore, do not consider this to be anything more than a guide and a book created for entertainment purposes.

The author and publisher are not liable or responsible for any damages or losses incurred by any person, which has allegedly been caused directly or indirectly by the information within this book.

If you do not agree with the above information, simply contact the author for a full refund.